Jesus Blesses the Children

written by KAREN COOLEY

illustrated by TERRY JULIEN

Taken from Luke 18:15-17

© 2006 Standard Publishing, Cincinnati, Ohio.
A division of Standex International Corporation. All rights reserved.
Printed in the United States of America.
Series design: Robert Glover. Cover and interior design: Steve Clark.
All Scripture quotations, unless otherwise indicated, are taken from
the Holy Bible, *New Living Translation*, copyright © 1996.
Used by permission of Tyndale House Publishers, Inc., Wheaton, Illinois 60189.
All rights reserved.

ISBN 0-7847-1930-6

12 11 10 09 08 07 06   9 8 7 6 5 4 3 2 1

Standard®
PUBLISHING
Bringing The Word to Life

Cincinnati, Ohio

"There he is, Mama! I see him! I see Jesus!"
Snatching his hand from his mother, the young boy
darted up the path.

"Come back here! Stay with us." Laughing, Mama turned to her daughter. "Run and catch up with your brother so he doesn't get into trouble."

Jesus had come to their town, and everyone was excited to see him! A crowd was already gathering to hear him speak.

Mama and Papa hurried to catch up to their children. As they got close to the crowd, they saw their children running toward a group of men.

Jesus was behind the men and the children were
having a hard time getting through.

"Hold on," a big man said angrily, stepping quickly in front of the children. "Leave Jesus alone! Don't bother him."

Tears filled the boy's eyes. Gently taking her brother's hand, the little girl quietly spoke. "Please, sir, we just want to see Jesus. We won't bother him."

By that time, Papa caught up to his children. Out of breath, he hurriedly said, "We just want Jesus to bless our children."

Other families crowded close. "Us, too," one mother said. "Can Jesus bless our children, too?"

Shocked at the boldness of these people, the man responded, "Jesus can't be bothered. Go away!"

Without another word to the families around them, the men turned their attention back to Jesus. They stood close to him, protecting him from the crowd.

Seeing that nothing else could be done, Papa hugged his little boy close and the family sadly turned to leave.

The family hadn't gone far when they heard a voice call out, "Wait!"

They turned around. It was Jesus! He was calling them! Maybe the men were wrong and Jesus really didn't mind if they brought their children to him. The little boy was so excited!

"Let the children come to me," Jesus said. "Don't stop them! For the Kingdom of God belongs to such as these. I assure you, anyone who doesn't have their kind of faith will never get into the Kingdom of God."

The men stepped aside so the families could get closer to Jesus. As they moved, the young boy's face lit up. His feet danced in delight. Finally he could see Jesus and get close enough to touch him!

Squealing with joy, the little boy ran toward Jesus, throwing himself into Jesus' open arms.

Other children followed right behind the boy, each receiving a hug and gentle touch from Jesus. Looking into each smiling face, Jesus blessed them. Joy shone in the eyes of the children. They knew they were special. Jesus loved them all very much.